Original title:
A House of Time

Copyright © 2025 Creative Arts Management OÜ
All rights reserved.

Author: Gideon Shaw
ISBN HARDBACK: 978-1-80587-190-3
ISBN PAPERBACK: 978-1-80587-660-1

Reflections in the Mirror

In the glass, a face grins wide,
Trying to remember why it tried.
Whispers of laughter, a twinge of cheer,
Yet the hair's gone wild, oh dear, oh dear!

Tick-tock goes the clock, it seems quite bold,
Chasing memories that never get old.
The mirror winks, it knows the score,
Who forgot to lock the front door?

Underneath the Eaves

Dust bunnies dance, quite the jig,
They hold a party, oh so big!
Under the eaves, they tell old tales,
Of socks and spoons lost in the gales.

A cat peeks in, with a puzzled meow,
"What's the agenda for fun right now?"
The dust bunnies cheer, with a fluffy delight,
Until the vacuum comes, oh what a fright!

The Lantern of Lost Time

A lantern flickers, in the attic's gloom,
Shadows of socks swirl, making room.
It's lit by wishes, all gone astray,
Oh, how they dance, then fade away!

The clock strikes three, though it's noon instead,
A slice of toast laughs at the crumbs it fed.
With giggles echoing, the lantern sways,
While yesterday's snacks still long for praise!

Threads of Yesterday

Each thread a story, woven tight,
From grandma's sweater, pink delight.
Yet the colors clash, a riot of hue,
Oh, what was she thinking? Not a clue!

In a corner waits a needle and grin,
Ready to stitch up all that's been.
But it starts to tangle, in a merry spree,
Creating a monster, oh what a sight to see!

Observing the Seasons

Spring arrives with a hop,
Flowers bloom and bugs plop.
Summer sizzles, ice cream drips,
Sunburns form on eager lips.

Autumn leaves take a dance,
Squirrels stash their nutty chance.
Winter wraps in frosty cheer,
Hot cocoa makes the fun appear.

The Frost of Forgotten Ages

Once a snowman stood so tall,
He melted fast, oh what a fall!
Forgotten in the garden's glow,
Now just a puddle, with nowhere to go.

Tales of frostbite and lost mittens,
Remembered when the cat once bitten.
They say pitchforks make great wands,
But it's best to avoid frost's bitter ponds.

Fractured Timepieces

Tick-tock goes the broken clock,
It thinks it's stuck in a rock.
Hours dance like they've had a fling,
Minutes jump – oh, what a thing!

A pendulum swings like it's lost its way,
Caught in a game of endless play.
Who knew clocks could wear such frowns?
When they lag behind, it's time to clown around!

The Echoes of Fading Days

Remembering when cats wore hats,
Chasing shadows of cheeky rats.
Old shoes with stories to tell,
Whisper echoes from a time we fell.

Dust bunnies hop, like they own the place,
While socks fight their own little race.
Days fade fast, but laughter stays,
In the echoes of our silliest ways.

The Portrait of Yesterday

In a frame that's slightly askew,
The past waves hello, then sneezes at you.
With socks that don't match and hair out of place,
Yesterday's portrait holds a gazing face.

It chuckles and giggles, what a grand affair,
As it dances around without much a care.
Telling tales of mischief, both silly and grand,
It spills all the secrets we can't understand.

Chasing Elastic Hours

The clock runs in circles, a very odd game,
While seconds stretch out, it's never the same.
I chase after minutes that wobble and squeak,
But they giggle away, so sly and so meek.

With springs that are bouncy and gears made of cheese,
Time slips through my fingers with childish ease.
I leap over tick-tock, I tumble and roll,
Elastic hours tease like a gummy bear's soul.

Rooms Filled with Moments

Step into the room, it's filled to the brim,
With giggles and grins on a whimsical whim.
There's laughter in corners, foot races in hall,
And timeouts for memories, come one, come all.

A chandelier swings on a rubber band thread,
While clocks in the corners giggle instead.
A pantry of laughter, a cupboard of fun,
In these silly rooms, life's never been done.

The Gears of Remembrance

The gears are quite rusty, but spinning with cheer,
They're squeaking out stories that tickle the ear.
With each little pop, a memory springs,
An orchestra playing all sorts of things.

Outrageous adventures tucked in each tooth,
Like a clumsy old wizard who forgets the truth.
They jive and they shimmy, those gears of delight,
Making moments seem wilder with each passing night.

A Path Through the Seasons

In spring, the flowers start to sneeze,
While winter blankets pine tree knees.
Summer's heat makes ice cream melt,
And autumn leaves dance, oh, what a felt!

A squirrel skates on icy ground,
It's a slippery mess, oh what a sound!
Chasing shadows in the noon glow,
Funny hats on scarecrows we know!

Midnight snacks in a hammock swing,
Chirping crickets at the twilight fling.
Seasons change like an outfit swap,
But laughter and fun—never stop!

Letters Stamped with Time

Each letter penned with giggles entwined,
Delivered by owls, oh how they whined.
In envelopes stamped with silly flares,
Whiskered cats reading with wise stares.

Postcards from pirates on strange high seas,
Requesting treasure to share 'til they sneeze.
Wishes wrapped in bubblegum strings,
Expecting joy—what joy that brings!

Time travels on a bicycle wheel,
With echoes of laughter, a wobbly feel.
Each note a riddle, wrapped up in rhyme,
Making the mundane feel like prime time!

The Architecture of Memory

Building blocks stacked high to the sky,
Each one wobbles—that's not a lie!
An igloo made of marshmallow fluff,
But one nibble and it's far too tough!

Rooms filled with giggles and silly debates,
In the hall of mirrors, we can't tell our fates.
Sketches of moments that break into smiles,
Dancing through corridors, oh, what miles!

Memory towers, some a bit crass,
With ghosts of mustaches made of grass.
Nostalgia sits in a comfy chair,
Wearing mismatched socks—how rarely fair!

Fading Echoes of Laughter

In the attic where shadows play,
Echoes of chuckles from yesterday.
Whispers of mischief hide in the nooks,
With dusty old books and soot-covered crooks.

A cat in a hat, a dog in a tie,
Trying to dance, oh my, oh my!
The floor creaks tales of who tripped when,
Each spill a story again and again.

Fading laughter from that old slide,
Where giggles and tumbles were a pride.
A symphony of joy wrapped in a bow,
With memories that twinkle like stars aglow!

Embracing the Unfurling

Leaves tangle like old friends,
Whispers sharing old tales.
Tick-tock, the clock shakes hands,
Cats wear clocks like cozy veils.

Dust bunnies dance in the light,
Sneaking behind the sofa's pride.
Time trips over its own shoes,
While socks play hide-and-seek, wide.

The fridge hums a sweet old song,
As leftovers waltz with zest.
Chairs gossip about the throng,
Of guests who always leave a mess.

Here laughter rings like a bell,
While bananas plot their escape.
In this realm where odd tales dwell,
Days unravel, oh what a shape!

A Tapestry of Time

Threadbare curtains catch the breeze,
While dust weaves tales of the past.
Each knot a story, frayed with ease,
As shadows yawn and stretch, unsurpassed.

Pots of gold in the attic gleam,
Worn-out shoes tell of toe-stubbing.
Time stitches dreams in a seam,
And the cat plots its own subbing.

Walls with whispers, secrets unfold,
Knobs that squeak like old men in jest.
Every tick of the clock feels bold,
As socks collect dust in their quest.

In this quilt where giggles roam,
And mismatched plates dance on the shelf,
Time swirls freely, calling it home,
While the clock rolls its eyes at itself.

The Sound of Silence

A creak echoes in the hall,
Mice gossip in quiet tones.
Worn-out chairs hold a ball,
Of laughter lingering like drones.

Spider webs hum a soft tune,
Tickled by drafts of hidden mirth.
Silent whispers of a raccoon,
Who claims the night for its own birth.

Clock hands play peekaboo games,
In the attic where echoes swell.
Silent moments shift like names,
As the old dog guards his spell.

Every nook hides a grin or two,
In this realm where stillness reigns.
Secrets giggle, always anew,
Amid the laughter, time attains.

Windows into Other Worlds

Framed views of odd, wild dreams,
Kites dance with unusually glee.
Next door's cat draws silly themes,
While wishing for endless sea.

Each window hides a little show,
A squirrel dressed as a chef.
Neighbors paint shadows in tow,
Sketching sides of time, quite deft.

Clouds drift like sandwiches caught,
In a whirlwind of curious whims.
Where is the time that we sought?
In laughter, it happily swims.

Peeking through panes brings delight,
To worlds where clocks can forget.
In this oddness, day turns night,
As dreams in giggles quietly met.

Whispers in the Hallway

When footsteps echo in the gloom,
I swear I hear a ghostly tune.
"What's for dinner?" they discuss,
I laugh aloud—who's making fuss?

They argue 'bout the socks I lost,
A mystery worth every cost.
In every creak, a tale unfolds,
Of treasures buried, stories told.

I sneak a peek where shadows roam,
Is it a specter or my gnome?
With playful banter, they unite,
In this old house, a comical sight.

My friends, both real and not so much,
Share their secrets with a touch.
Together we all laugh away,
In the hall, we dance and play.

The Ticking Walls

The clocks conspire, they tick and tock,
Each one in place—a stubborn rock.
They joke about my lack of speed,
As I forget each task and deed.

I swear the wall's an eager host,
Dinner's served, yet I just roast.
They nudge me, 'Time is up, old chap!'
I'm still asleep, caught in the nap.

The pendulums swing, a waltzing pair,
Teasing me with their constant stare.
I wave them off with playful cheer,
As they chime loudly—"Get over here!"

They giggle each hour, the sly old things,
While I just wish for the time springs.
Why rush now? Let laughter unwind,
In this race through time, joy I'll find.

portraits of a Past Life

On the wall, they grin and stare,
Framed expressions full of flair.
They whisper secrets, tales of old,
Of lives lived loud, adventures bold.

A mustached man with a classy hat,
Claims he danced with a furry cat.
While grandma laughs—her story's fish,
She caught a whale, she swears—oh, delish!

They share their quirks and quirky charms,
To bring me joy with all their arms.
"Don't mind the dust, it's just our vibe,"
"They may be early, but we arrived!"

With every glance, another jest,
In faded frames, they seem so blessed.
Living portraits, always near,
In joyful chatter, I find my cheer.

Time's Silent Keeper

A friendly face in every room,
The keeper smiles, dispels the gloom.
He has no rush, he takes it slow,
With quiet laughs as time will flow.

He gathers moments like fine wine,
Each cork a tale, they intertwine.
"Just sit right back, enjoy the ride,"
He says with warmth, no need to hide.

"Remember, jokes are just like clock,
They tick and tock, and sometimes shock!"
His wisdom drips like honeyed tea,
"Embrace the waits, be wild and free."

So here's to time, the keeper dear,
Let's celebrate with smiles, not fear.
With every tick, he twirls in dance,
In every giggle, we take a chance.

Shadows of Dust

In corners thick with whispering air,
Old socks play tag without a care.
The clock mocks me with its tick-tock,
While dust bunnies dance, oh what a shock!

Grandma's chair gives a creak and a sigh,
I swear it's plotting my next pie dye.
Time wiggles its toes on the floor mat,
While the cat judges me, how very (un)fat!

The Pulse of Timelessness

The toaster dings like a doorbell ring,
As I toast my hopes, the kitchen sings.
The fridge hums tunes of buttery dreams,
While I chase leftovers, or so it seems.

The vacuum shouts out, 'Don't tread on me!',
As I dance with the broom in wild glee.
A calendar notes my procrastination,
It fills me with dread and elation!

Candlelight and Echoes

In twilight's glow, shadows juggle around,
As I trip over history, laughter's profound.
The chandelier sways, with a giggle it clinks,
While echoes of secrets spill out of the sinks.

Ghosts of my past throw an awkward soirée,
They dance in their slippers, no serious play.
Candlelight flickers, it's hosting a show,
As I snicker at memories I've come to outgrow!

Remnants of an Era

Old magazines, with faces askew,
Whispering secrets of a time we once knew.
The sofa spills stories of snacks and of friends,
While the TV debates its own channels and bends.

Under the rug, the dust bunnies huddle,
Planning a revolution, oh such a cuddle!
Time is a prankster, it teases us well,
In the remnants of times, where laughter does dwell!

A Tangle of Voices

In the attic, whispers cheer,
Dusty secrets, clamor near.
Old socks chuckle, light a fire,
Ticking clocks tease, never tire.

Mices debate who stole the cheese,
Curtains gossip with the breeze.
Odd socks dance a jolly jig,
Under the bed, they play a gig.

Grandma's chair exhibits flair,
In her lap, a cat lays fair.
The lampshade gives a wink or two,
While the fridge hums like a tune.

Time's a jester, funny mask,
Never known for being 'ask'.
Laughter echoes through the halls,
In this place, no one falls!

The Calendar of Longing

Each page flips with a silly grin,
Days of week dressed in a spin.
Monday grumpy, Tuesday bright,
Wednesday's midweek dance delight.

Holidays toss confetti high,
While weeks just wave and say goodbye.
Time wears glasses, grows a beard,
With every tick, it seems so weird.

November's turkey tries to fly,
While April's showers laugh and cry.
Time's a prankster, don't you see?
Juggling months, he's quite the spree.

Circled dates are lost in the fun,
Future jokes told by the sun.
In this dance of wibbly woo,
Each second whispers, "I love you!"

In the Nooks of Yesterday

In the corners where shadows play,
Yesterday's jokes still laugh away.
Old radio hums a jazzy tune,
Dust bunnies twirl beneath the moon.

Framed moments wink with delight,
Stale popcorn holds on to the night.
Time giggles in an empty chair,
A donut's crumbs fly everywhere.

Saggy couches have stories to tell,
Tales of laughter, how they fell.
In this nook where echoes reside,
Funny faces sneak and hide.

Nostalgia dances on the wall,
Whispered laughs, an endless call.
In this realm where memories gleam,
Time's a twiddle, a cheeky dream!

Navigating Through Time's Maze

A corridor bends and shakes with cheer,
Lively lamps laugh with the passing year.
Each door opens with a squeak,
In each cupboard, giggles peek.

Turning left, a shimmer awaits,
Right, a ghost plays with the plates.
Time's a compass that spins around,
In this labyrinth, joy is found.

Calendars skate on rollerblades,
Jumpy clocks spill their time cascades.
With peeking grins, they race and run,
Welcome to the maze of fun!

With each twist and every turn,
You'll discover more, oh how you'll yearn.
Time's a maze for playful hearts,
In its corners, laughter starts!

The Yielding of Memories

In corners where dust bunnies dance,
Old socks hold lengthy romance.
Each cup a witness to spilled dreams,
While the fridge hums forgotten themes.

Lamps flicker like they've lost their sight,
Chasing shadows by the pale moonlight.
The clock ticks loud, but no one cares,
Time's in a race with mismatched chairs.

Tongues wagging from portraits hung,
The dog rolls eyes at jokes once sung.
Lost remotes have conversations grand,
As they plot a heist to take the land.

In the laughter of ghosts, we find glee,
Beneath the dust, they still have tea.
Memories yield a playful chime,
In this quirky, timeless paradigm.

Ghosts of Past Whispers

In the attic, a chair seems to sigh,
Cushions tell tales of days gone by.
Photographs whisper with a grin,
As the wallpaper blushes with sin.

The clock hands conspire to take a trip,
Chasing echoes in a playful blip.
A cat appears, sporting a crown,
While dust motes waltz in a swirl around.

Hooks hang stories of misfit elks,
In jackets too snug for household helks.
Ghosts play chess on the kitchen floor,
Laughing at moves that no one saw before.

Time giggles loud like a child at play,
With secrets tucked neatly in yesterday.
In this realm where mischief abounds,
Past whispers cheer with echoing sounds.

Rituals of the Forgotten

Under beds, the shoes have a bash,
Plotting their exit with a secret stash.
The broom scoffs at the dust it must keep,
While the vacuum plots its next big leap.

Old coats scheme in the hall by the door,
Arguing over their last big score.
The rug rolls its eyes, but it can't flee,
As popcorn fights with the TV spree.

A rubber chicken makes an odd demand,
For a dance party; it takes the stand.
While pots and pans join in the fun,
Adding rhythm until the day is done.

Memories gather like cackling hens,
In the warmth of laughter, where joy transcends.
These forgotten rituals twist and play,
Creating glee in the silliest way.

The Embrace of Shadows

Shadows giggle in the evening light,
Stretching their arms, what a whimsical sight!
The couch gives in with a creaking sound,
As cushions conspire to jump from the ground.

Floors that squeak sing tales so bright,
While cobwebs wave their goodnight.
The mirror winks with a knowing cheer,
Reflecting laughter that only we hear.

Boxes of treasures rattle away,
As their contents come out to play.
A hat spins stories of times so dire,
With hiccups of humor and sparks of fire.

In this space where joy tends to grow,
With each silly dance, the wonders flow.
Shadows embrace with a giggle divine,
In the realm of whimsy, where all is fine.

The Staircase of Ages

Up we go, with squeaky steps,
Each stair a laugh, where time has crept.
Old socks and shoes, they start to dance,
As history twirls in a silly prance.

Beneath the light, dust bunnies play,
Telling tales of yesterday.
They leap and hop with every grin,
Who knew time could be so thin?

Wobbly frames of furniture talk,
Sharing secrets of a long lost walk.
With every creak, a chuckle's found,
A staircase that just spins around.

So grab a snack, and please don't trip,
Join the chase in this funny trip.
For up and down we'll laugh away,
In this odd house where we will stay.

Echoes of Laughter

In corners where the whispers play,
Echos bounce in a comical array.
Ghosts of giggles fill the room,
Bringing smiles, dispelling gloom.

A rubber chicken on the shelf,
Mimics joy of a youthful self.
Tickling memories, the walls do sway,
In this laughter's grand ballet.

Every tick of the clock, a joke,
Turning serious moments to a poke.
As shadows dance, time's tricks we find,
Echoes of laughter, never behind.

So let's turn the frown into a grin,
With each cheeky chime, we dive right in.
In this quirky time, we shall reside,
Where humor and heart forever abide.

Dust and Daydreams

The dust floats high in the afternoon,
Dancing dumbly to an olden tune.
With every swoosh, they brush our dreams,
Making mishaps out of mundane schemes.

Socks that wander, shoes that weep,
Tangled tales where chuckles leap.
Daydreams fly through windows wide,
Chasing giggles with every glide.

Crumbs of snacks lay here and there,
Winking slyly, a tasty affair.
With each quick nap, we set the stage,
For a show that spans the ages.

So let's name the dust with a new rhyme,
A playful pact between space and time.
In this place of oddities, we find reprieve,
As joy and surprise weave in what we believe.

Lost Hours, Found Places

Time slips by in funny ways,
Lost in laughter, found in plays.
A clock that giggles with every tick,
Bending rules, just for the trick.

Under the beds where dust bunnies roam,
We find the laughter that's always home.
Each lost hour, a treasure unfold,
As silly stories are told and retold.

The walls are lined with silly chatter,
Memories made that endlessly splatter.
From breakfast hiccups to bedtime sings,
Every moment, joyfully clings.

So let's stumble through this timeless race,
With every smile that lights up a face.
In this wondrous world of giggles and grace,
We'll find our home in every place.

Chambers of the Forgotten

In a room where the dust bunnies play,
Old socks whisper secrets of yesterday.
A chair that squeaks like it's got quite a tale,
Of how it once supported a cat and a whale.

Cracks in the walls hold giggles from years,
Echoing laughter through clinks of old beers.
The lightbulb flickers like a dance gone awry,
As memories tumble and come out to sigh.

The Clockwork Heart

Tick-tock goes the heart in a comical race,
With gears that wobble and a curious face.
It laughs at the minutes, trips on the hours,
Trying to measure the joy of the flowers.

Each second a riddle, each minute a joke,
As the pendulum swings like a whimsical bloke.
In a spurt of tickles, it turns back the time,
And dances to rhythms, both silly and sublime.

Stories in the Attic

In the attic, where oddities thrive,
A hat with a feather and a once great hive.
Dusty old boxes, each holds a new prank,
With curtains of cobwebs that laugh as they stank.

The trunk plays the joker, the chair cracks a grin,
While a ghostly old lamp does a jig with a spin.
Old toys all chime in, with stories to weave,
Of adventures gone wild, no adult can believe.

The Garden of Seasons

In a garden where seasons all mingle and blend,
The flowers gossip and giggle, my friend.
Spring tells a joke that makes winter roll,
While summer suns in on the punchline's whole goal.

Autumn throws leaves like confetti all around,
As winter just grumbles, 'Don't make a sound!'
Each bloom wears a hat, the herbs throw a feast,
In this patch of hilarity, laughter won't cease.

The Weaving of Time's Tapestry

In the attic, dust bunnies prance,
Old clocks giggle, given a chance.
Knitting yarn of moments past,
With each stitch, a memory cast.

Grandpa's beard, a tangled mess,
Timelines twist with each caress.
A spool of laughter rolls amok,
As time winks from the grandfather clock.

Each thread is a tale, funny and bright,
Like socks that vanished in the night.
Seasons laugh, their colors combine,
In this fabric, the absurd will shine.

So let's dance in this woven jest,
Time's silly game is simply the best.
With each tangle, we gleefully climb,
In this quilt of chaos, we find our rhyme.

Doors Open to Tomorrow

A door creaks with a chuckling sound,
Behind it, my lost socks are found.
Past the threshold, giggles collide,
With a calendar where cats can't hide.

Step right through to yesterday's mess,
Panels shift, and I must confess.
That door marked "Wednesday" swung too wide,
Now it's Thursday, and I've lost my ride.

A whirlwind of moments spirals about,
Funny how time can twist and tout.
With each knob turned, I bump my head,
Into futures where no one's fed.

But what's the rush in a bumpy race?
Tomorrow's a joke with a smiling face.
With a leap and a laugh, I rush ahead,
To see what chaos my dreams have bred.

Ancestral Footsteps

Grandpa's shoes are huge and bright,
In them, I trip, what a silly sight!
An echo of laughter fills the air,
As I tumble, unaware and rare.

Ancestors dance in coats so old,
Their stories shimmer, a sight to behold.
With each step, a whoosh and a puff,
Life's a garden, but sometimes rough.

Grandma's hat is perched askew,
Every glance tells me what to do.
In family tales, we all take part,
Time jests as we play the heart.

Through patchwork stories, we boldly stride,
With every slip, we can't help but glide.
Ancestral footsteps, one silly chase,
In this joyful dance, we find our place.

The Pendulum's Dance

A pendulum swings with a silly grin,
Tick-tock teasing, come on in!
Back and forth like a dance of youth,
It winks at seconds, oh what a truth!

With each sway, it cracks a joke,
Time's a prankster that never chokes.
It taps its toes on a vibrant beat,
Making minutes feel like a treat.

As it boogies through the day,
It seems to laugh in a playful way.
A hiccup of hours, a giggle-filled hour,
Time sprouts flowers, claiming its power.

So let's waltz with this time-slinging friend,
Laughter and moments, they blissfully blend.
For in this dance where we twirl and whirl,
Time's strange rhythm makes our heads swirl.

Nightfall in the Living Room

The couch declares it's time for naps,
While socks unite in mismatched maps.
A cat on the carpet, dreams of a race,
Chasing shadows in a time looped space.

The clock ticks loudly like a cheesy clock,
While popcorn pop sings, with a playful knock.
Each game forgotten, each laugh a surprise,
As the TV giggles, slipping through lies.

Lamp shades waltz with a flickering glow,
The table hums tunes from long ago.
But the fridge holds secrets, ice cream divine,
In the nightfall's realm where we all dine.

Yet as slumber creeps in, dreams mouse through the door,

Whispering tales of what came before.
The living room chuckles, with mischievous grace,
A comical party where no one's in place.

The Corridor of Forgotten Dreams

In the hallway, echoes of laughter clink,
Where shadows parade and candle flames wink.
Forgotten dreams housed in frames askew,
They roll their eyes like they've seen it all too.

Shoes on the floor gossip about their trips,
While dust bunnies gather, sharing old quips.
Each door a portal to yesterdays wild,
The corridor chuckles, a mischievous child.

Pictures smirk down, with knowing grins bright,
As they swap tales of the exhilarating flight.
A broom in the corner daydreams of dance,
Trying so hard to give dust one last chance.

But whispers tumble, their secrets unfold,
In this corridor where time's never old.
It leads to adventures with each swaying swing,
A magical marathon, oh what laughs they bring!

Encounters with Time

Watches twirl in dizzy delight,
Ticking jokes that dance through the night.
Moments stroll by with a wobbly gait,
In this whimsical world where seconds wait.

Old calendars chuckle, their dates all askew,
Playing hide and seek with the days that flew.
Each second a prankster, each minute a laugh,
As they race against clocks in this timeless craft.

Sundials gossip in the warm sunshine,
While hourglasses waste sand, pretending they're fine.
"Catch us if you can!" time playfully shouts,
As it tumbles and tumbles, revealing its routes.

But when night hits, the shadows convene,
Creating a ruckus, a time-travel scene.
They bounce and they jiggle, in dim twilight,
Making fun of the hours till the morning light.

The Breath of Eras

In the attic resides a gentle sigh,
Old toys telling tales as they float by.
A whisper of laughter, a ghost in disguise,
As time takes a breath, while the present complies.

Each relic a jester, wearing faded clothes,
Juggling memories from ages that froze.
A rocking chair creaks with stories to text,
While the dust balls dance, oh, what a perplex!

Old clocks in the corner chime softly with glee,
Swapping their tales for a cup of hot tea.
They stretch the minutes, twist hours with flair,
In this space where laughter hangs thick in the air.

So let's toast to the moments, the snickers and grins,
To the breath of the eras and the chaos it spins.
For in this laughter-filled bubble we find,
The joy of the past is forever entwined.

Time's Parlor of Dreams

In a room where clocks all chime,
And dust bunnies dance to the rhyme.
The sofa sneezes, the rug kicks back,
As furniture swaps tales from a crack.

A cat is napping on a old chair,
Whispers of laughter float through the air.
Tea spills while the kettle sings loud,
In a parlor where time's never cowed.

The wallpaper peels out a joke,
As the lightbulb flickers, a chuckle it woke.
Candles giggle in their waxy embrace,
In this timeless place, there's always a race.

Ghosts of socks hide under the bed,
Where slippers and crutches have all been fed.
With tick-tock humor and giggles galore,
This silly abode has much to explore.

Handprints of Antiquity

Dusty corners hold secrets so tight,
Where handprints mingle with laughter at night.
The old rocking chair creaks a sweet tune,
While shadows play tag under the moon.

Grandma's cat naps on the old quilt,
While time slips by without any guilt.
Spoonfuls of chuckles held tight in a jar,
With cookies that vanished where sweet dreams are.

A clock with a grin counts seconds with glee,
As the fridge hums jokes, it's a real jubilee.
Chipped tea cups share whispers of cheer,
As moths flutter by in their antique sphere.

Old photos wink from the dusty wood,
Each frame a story that's somehow good.
This dwelling is silly, a palace of cheer,
Where handprints of yore flourish year after year.

Patterns in Stillness

In stillness, the patterns swirl round,
A living room dance, without a sound.
The carpet throws shapes, it twists with glee,
While curtains gossip, oh do they see!

Chairs aren't just objects, they've got a soul,
Telling their truths, making time roll.
The old lamp nods in its vintage flair,
As the couch chuckles, a comfy affair.

The calendar giggles at dates long past,
While the dust motes tango, oh what a blast!
Windows peek in on the silliness churned,
In patterns of stillness, life's lessons learned.

And although silence is woven in seams,
It dances and wiggles through all of our dreams.
This crazy abode, with patterns galore,
In stillness, it hums with stories and more.

A Tenancy of Memories

In a curious place filled with doodles and quips,
Where echoes of laughter take curious trips.
The fridge is a sage, with stories to share,
While spoons and forks giggle in rhythmic despair.

Each wall holds a memory, each corner a grin,
As chairs and tables spin tales from within.
Mismatched socks argue over who'll fold,
In this hodgepodge house where hugs turn to gold.

With playful ghosts making mischief by night,
The bathroom mirror reports every slight.
Old shoes chant ballads that no one can hear,
As this tenancy thrives on love and good cheer.

So let's celebrate this glorious mess,
With heartbeats and chuckles, no room for distress.
In a sweet little haven, memories entwine,
And silliness swirls to the rhythm of time.

When Walls Could Speak

If these walls could tell a tale,
They'd laugh and giggle without fail.
Echoes of sneezes and cat's wild prance,
A tribute to the awkward dance.

With every crack, a memory's wink,
Like the time I forgot to blink.
A ghost with a penchant for bad puns,
Stealing my socks and having fun.

Chasing dust bunnies 'round the room,
Critiquing my choice of flower bloom.
"Oh, dear friend, what a sight you've made!"
Walls would chuckle, unafraid.

So here's to whispers, loud and clear,
In my home filled with joy and cheer!
If only these walls had a voice,
They'd tell of laughter, oh what a choice!

Shadows of Time Past

In corners dark, the shadows play,
Whispering secrets from yesterday.
A sock, a shoe, the odd lost glove,
What will they say? It's all a shove!

Tick-tock echoes, quite a tease,
"Remember that time you lost your keys?"
They dance around like cheeky sprites,
Leading me on wild, silly flights.

"Oh, those dishes piled high!" they sigh,
"Will they ever reach the sky?"
A feline pauses in the deed,
A grand observer, yes indeed.

Time rolls on with jovial glee,
In shadows deep, there's joy, you see!
For every flicker, every glance,
Memories join this silly dance!

The Weaving of Timelines

Threads of laughter, colors bold,
Weaving stories sweet and old.
In a tapestry of joy and woe,
Each stitch a tale, let's start the show!

Loops of mischief and little lies,
Like the time I wore mismatched ties.
The fabric stretches, flips, and swirls,
A patchwork made of giggling pearls.

Grandma's wisdom, a knot so tight,
"Don't trust your memory!" she'd ignite.
But every fray tells of mishaps chaste,
Each thread a moment not to waste.

So here's to weaving with laughter and cheer,
Stitching our way through the passing years!
With every pull, we craft a rhyme,
In this merry dance through the fabric of time!

Memories in a Jar

I took my memories, put them away,
In a jar marked 'funny', for a rainy day.
Each moment a giggle, a slip, a fall,
A sunset barbecue, my best friend's call.

A lid so tight, but laughter sneaks through,
Like the time I wore two shoes askew.
"Let's pour some joy, a dash of delight!"
With a sprinkle of quirks, we'll make it bright.

Each time I open, the chuckles abound,
With dreams of sunshine and awkward sounds.
"Who knew memories could be so nice?
Life's little mishaps, a platter of spice!"

So here's to jars, both large and small,
Filled with laughter, and love for all!
Seal them tight, but don't forget to share,
For memories in jars, are rare flair!

Remnants in the Walls

In the attic, dust bunnies dance,
With secrets and odd bits, they prance.
Old shoes hang by a thread so thin,
Wonder if they ever made a win!

A calendar upside down, how fine,
Marks birthdays and days without a sign.
The wallpaper chuckles, peels a bit,
Echoes of laughter where kids used to sit.

Nostalgia in the floorboards creak,
Whispers of ages, they start to speak.
Latin verbs, calculus woes,
Ghosts of homework in every doze!

In the cellar, pickles sing out loud,
Jarred memories, oh so proud.
Socks from the dryer lend a hand,
Plotting adventures in their own band.

Time's Unseen Threads

In the closet, ties knotted tight,
Argue who wore which on what night.
The sweaters grumble, moths seek a feast,
Wishing for warmth, not an added beast!

The grandfather clock snores with grace,
Time never rushes, finds its own pace.
Tick-tock tattoos on the wall's face,
Each second it tickles – a wobbly race!

Old toys huddle, gossip the past,
Wonder if they'll outlast the cast.
The rubber duckies, proud in their space,
Paddle through memories like a slow chase!

Postcards stuck where the sun don't shine,
Tell tales of beaches, lost in a line.
The pen's ink laughs, drip-drop remark,
At dreams still waiting beyond the park.

The Threads of Memory

Grandma's quilt holds stories tight,
Stitched in colors, a patchwork delight.
Each square a memory, we giggle and sigh,
Like ice cream running – oh me, oh my!

Downstairs, the fridge hums a tune,
Dreams of snacks by the light of the moon.
Celery sticks wearing capes of cheese,
Join in on rumbles that never cease.

The clock in the hall, a trickster bold,
Always goes backward, never grows old.
Laughing at 'later', 'now', and 'soon',
It trades its hands for a silly cartoon!

Where's that cat? In a sunbeam, a king,
Judging our time, what joy it can bring.
As night creeps in with pearls on a thread,
Whispers of bedtime scurry to bed!

Revelations in the Quiet

Under the stairs, a concert of creaks,
Whispering secrets in hushed little tweaks.
The broom in the corner plays jazz so sweet,
While the dustpan keeps rhythm, tapping its feet.

Chairs spin stories, old wood with flair,
A parade of mishaps that no one would dare.
With gum under the seat, a sticky affair,
The laughter of youth floats up in the air!

Meals gone by in whispers and sighs,
The gravy boat winks from under the pies.
Each plate contains tales of feasts and fun,
Echoes of everyone when day was just done.

In the shadows, a sunset hides well,
Echoing laughter like a distant bell.
In quiet corners where dreams lie awake,
The humor of time is all that we make.

Staircases of History

On staircases creaky and old,
History whispers tales bold.
A sandwich lost in the fray,
Maybe it's time for some play!

With every step, I hear a tale,
Of knights who danced and ships set sail.
A rogue with a wig, oh so grand,
Juggles secrets with a hand!

The walls giggle with ancient lore,
As cats in cloaks sneak out the door.
A laugh erupts from the past,
Did I just see a ghost run fast?

So let's slide down this winding track,
To where the laughter pulls us back.
In socks or slippers, take your stance,
And tumble through history's dance!

The Embrace of Twilight

At twilight's fall, we giggle and sway,
Under stars and the moon's soft play.
The clocks are winking, oh what a sight,
Time forgot to set it right!

In the corner, shadows start a fight,
A chair declares, "You're not my type!"
The sun dips low, wearing a frown,
While the moon wears glitter and a crown.

Crickets chirp in a humorous tune,
A fridge hums like the old raccoon.
In every corner, laughter's spun,
As if twilight is having too much fun.

So let the colors dance and craze,
While time in twilight does its maze.
We'll twirl and twist until we drop,
In this embrace, we'll never stop!

In the Halls of Chronos

In the halls where time begins to slide,
Wacky clocks do a goofy glide.
A minute here, a second there,
Tick tock laughs float through the air!

I'll trade my watch for a silly hat,
Join a debate with a curious cat.
"What's the time?" bumbles the old clock,
"Just a moment!" with a hearty knock!

The walls murmur with chimes so sweet,
An echo from the past, can't be beat.
With every tick, there's a comic cheer,
Chronos winks and whispers, "I'm here!"

So dance with seconds, let laughter ring,
In the halls where absurdity sings.
For every tick marks a moment new,
And the best of time is shared with you!

Timeless Corners of the Heart

In the attic, dust bunnies play,
Chasing memories that start to sway.
Old photographs line the wall,
Each one grins, but none can recall.

The clock ticks loud, a snicker in glee,
It whispers tales of what used to be.
Socks mismatched, a sign of my style,
Left behind, but covers a smile.

In the cupboard, a jar of old jelly,
It wobbles and jiggles, quite almost smelly.
Butterflies dance on yellow wallpaper,
Every flutter a tiny caper.

There's laughter hidden under the stairs,
Where no one checks, it's full of bears.
Each corner twinkles with silly charm,
In this space, your heart feels warm.

Fragments of a Fleeting Hour

Time slips through like sand in a glass,
It tickles the toes, then it's gone fast.
Old tea cups whisper tales of cheer,
They toast to moments, precious and dear.

The clock's a prankster, it skips a beat,
Sipping on echoes, a delicious treat.
Laughter bounces off the ceiling high,
While shadows pretend not to sigh.

In the garden, weeds wear crowns of gold,
Their reign, however, is cheekily bold.
A gnome winks, planted just for fun,
Each flower giggles, it's always a run.

As the sun dips low, and shadows meld,
The tales of the hour are finally held.
Twirling like dancers, time takes its bow,
Forever stealing the laughter now.

The Dust of Ages

In corners where sunlight refuses to creep,
Layers of dust have secrets to keep.
Each grain a story, a giggle, a cheer,
Collecting laughter from yesteryear.

Dusty old books hold wonders inside,
With covers that grin and pages that hide.
They flutter and flap, performing their plays,
While dust motes dance in a timeless ballet.

The chandelier swings, a clumsy old thing,
It jangles with joy when the cat starts to spring.
Laughter cascades as the glasses all clink,
Old spirits join in with a wink and a wink.

In twilight's embrace, we ponder the day,
In the dust of ages, we laugh, dance, and sway.
With echoes of time caught in each little rush,
Life's a funny story wrapped in a hush.

Lullabies of Lost Youth

In the backyard, a swing creaks with cheer,
It sings lullabies we long to hear.
A seesaw's giggle, a child's quick dash,
Remnants of laughter from a joyful splash.

Marbles are treasures, shiny and bright,
Rolling away like memories of flight.
The jump rope whispers, "Come, jump with me!"
In circles of joy, we're forever free.

A bicycle waits, tires flat on the ground,
Its stories of races forever abound.
In faded old sneakers, we danced through the hall,
Each step a reminder, we're young after all.

With twilight's arrival, the fireflies glow,
They twirl through the air, a whimsical show.
Lullabies echo in the soft evening light,
In the heart of the night, we hold on tight.

The Library of Lost Dreams

In a corner, a book with no cover,
Whispers secrets of the lost and the lovers.
Pages flutter like confused birds,
Hiding tales that seem quite absurd.

Dust bunnies dance on the empty shelves,
Trying to read books about other selves.
A novel titled 'How to Nap Well',
Just might be the best buy to sell.

Check-out clerks are turtles, you see,
They take forever, it's quite the spree.
Hold your breath for the punchline drop,
As the last sentence makes you flop.

So gather your dreams, never too late,
Even if they're trapped behind an old gate.
In this library, laughter's the theme,
Where every lost dream becomes a meme.

Fragments of the Unraveling

In the attic, a tapestry hangs,
Threads of laughter now live with the fangs.
Each knot's a memory, a jab at the past,
Where time's sense of humor is unsurpassed.

A half-spun sweater, marked by a sigh,
Worn by Grandma with a wink in her eye.
She said, 'Dress warm, but don't be a clown!',
Yet clowns walk the streets of a sleepy old town.

Tick-tock goes the clock with a giggle,
Tickling time like a child's silly wiggle.
Fragments of moments caught in the chase,
As time spins in circles, lost in a race.

So unravel the laughter, let memories stick,
In the fabric of life, find the punchy slick.
Each thread tells a tale that's oddly defined,
In this chaotic yarn of the jester's mind.

Guardians of the Gilded Clock

Behold the clock with its golden sheen,
Guardians chuckle, they're quite the scene.
Timekeepers fumble the hands 'round and 'round,
Fumbling time like it's lost and found.

Chimes sound like a cat with a sore throat,
While clocks race each other in a comical float.
One tick-tocks wildly, the other just stops,
It's a race to the finish with flip-flap hops.

Statues blink slowly as time drips like goo,
'Can you believe the things we've been through?'
The gears all groan with a rusty delight,
As moments collide in a humorous fight.

So cherish the chaos in every tick-tock,
Where fun fills the air, and jokes gently rock.
The guardians grinning, on duty all day,
Keeping the laughter not too far away.

The Foyer of Memories

Step into the foyer, a quirky affair,
Where shoes of the past mingle with air.
A lost sock lingers, with stories to tell,
Of midnight escapades gone wonderfully well.

Coats whisper secrets beneath the old rack,
'Are you coming back, or just taking a crack?'
Footprints laugh, and they skedaddle about,
Tickling the toes of those coming out.

Mirrors reflect what they just could not see,
Echoing giggles of fond anarchy.
Frames hold the snapshots of joy and disguise,
As memories dance with twinkling eyes.

So take a step back and enjoy the view,
In this jolly foyer, the past sings to you.
Every corner a tale, every shoe a belief,
In the laughter of life, discover your relief.

Whispers of the Past

In the attic, dust bunnies play,
Whispering tales of an olden day.
A cat with a hat, oh what a sight,
Chasing shadows, in the moonlight.

Grandma's chair with a creak and groan,
Complains of all the time it's known.
Every cushion holds a chuckle or two,
As the sofa asks, where did you go?

The mirror grins with a wink and a nod,
Reflecting faces that feel quite odd.
"Is that you, or just my cousin Fred?"
"I lost my hair, but not my dread!"

Photographs dance on the kitchen wall,
Each frozen smile, a funny sprawl.
Time tickles us in the silliest way,
Oh, the stories we laugh about today!

The Clock's Secret Chamber

In the corner sits a clock so bold,
Ticking tales that never grow old.
Its face is smiling, it's hiding a tune,
A serenade sung by a grumpy raccoon.

Behind the hands, a party is found,
With dancing spoons and a trumpet sound.
Time is sassy, it'll make you giggle,
As gears play hopscotch and softly wiggle.

Each hour strikes with a whimsical flair,
The minutes wiggle, without a care.
"Oh dear, I'm late!" says the second hand,
"Off to the dance, oh isn't it grand?"

So come join the fun, give time a cheer,
In the clock's chamber, there's nothing to fear.
Just laughter and joy, as the hands keep time,
Where seconds can shuffle and rhythm can rhyme!

Windows to Forgotten Days

Peeking through the glass, a view so wide,
Of laughter and chaos on the other side.
A dog in sunglasses rides a bike,
Chasing the postman, oh what a hike!

Every window shows a tale or two,
Of silly antics that once flew.
A scarecrow wearing a feathered hat,
Trying to dance, but oh he fell flat!

The curtains sway like they're part of the scene,
Whispering jokes from a time machine.
"Is that a sock? Or a hat on a frog?"
"Both!" they laugh, "What an odd dialogue!"

So peek through the panes, let your giggles out,
Each frame is a joke, there's never a doubt.
In windows of whimsy, find laughter anew,
In forgotten days, where silliness grew!

Timekeeper's Reverie

Oh, the timekeeper snoozes, what a sight!
Counting sheep that dance in the night.
Tick-tock, tick-tock, they jump and prance,
In dreams where clocks wear pants and dance.

"Time flies!" they shout with a wink and a grin,
Chasing the seconds, and spinning in sin.
With armfuls of moments, they stack and they play,
Building a castle where giggles hold sway.

A pendulum swings with a chuckle so deep,
While hours do somersaults, never sleep.
"Oh dear, I'm stuck!" cries the silly old gear,
"I lost my place in this fun atmosphere!"

So let's raise a toast to the tick-tock crew,
For time's just a jest, and it's all about you.
In this merry reverie, let laughter unfold,
For each passing minute, there's humor to hold!

Reflection in a Glass Bottle

Once I found a bottle bright,
It reflected me—what a sight!
I laughed at my goofy face,
A funhouse mirror in this space.

Inside it swirled my lunch from noon,
A medley of soup, a soggy boon.
Is this a portal to another realm?
Or just my snack at the helm?

The bottle giggled with each jig,
Telling tales, both large and big.
I pondered if I'd found a friend,
Who'd share my jokes until the end.

But alas, my snack was just a tease,
A fleeting muse in gusts of breeze.
I tipped it back, gave it a chug,
Giggled as it became a drug.

Patterns of Sunlight and Shadow

Sunlight dances on the floor,
Twirling like it wants to soar.
Shadows stretch in playful fight,
Poking fun at golden light.

A shadow puppet takes a bow,
An elephant! No, it's a cow!
I twirl and laugh in this bright game,
While sunlight blushes, feeling lame.

Patterns shift like hats in wind,
Cactus hats or spoons? Who's pinned?
As light and dark create a scene,
My room becomes a comic screen.

So next time shadows start to play,
Join them in their funky ballet.
For in this tale of light and shade,
Every giggle must be made.

The Silence Between Seconds

Tick-tock, the clock does mock,
Whispers in a secret stock.
What if time held back a grin,
And seconds laughed, tucked within?

I listened close, beneath the sound,
A giggle here, a chuckle found.
Each second nudged the next with glee,
"Can you believe? We're wild and free!"

Moments collide, create a mess,
Here's some joy, and here's the stress.
Each tick a joke, each tock a tease,
Life's a comedy, if you please.

So let them laugh, let moments dance,
Each second's winks invite romance.
In silence, find the fun implied,
The sweetest jokes we cannot hide.

Forgotten Corners of Eternity

In a corner, dust bunnies play,
They've formed a band, hip-hop ballet!
Eternity rolls its eyes, bemused,
At rabbits lost, but still amused.

Forgotten socks, where do they roam?
In socktopia, they've made a home!
With matching pairs lost in the fray,
They dance and jiggle away all day.

Old memories sit like chairs in shade,
Trying to remember the jokes they made.
Each laugh like wind, both soft and light,
Echoes through corners, just out of sight.

So when you peek in shadows dim,
Quite possible, you'll join their whim.
For timeless fun waits patiently,
In the corners of what's yet to be.

Faded Photographs

Old snapshots hiding in a dusty drawer,
Their colors laugh as they ask for more.
Uncle Bob's hair was a wild orange blaze,
His mustache outsmarts all the latest fads.

Grandma knitting in a fashionable cap,
But the dog wore it better, a furry chap.
Uncle Joe's dancing, a sight to behold,
Two left feet make the stories more bold.

The cat grins wide from the yellowed page,
A timeless giggle from a hilarious stage.
Just look at that smile, so out of control,
Memories linger—oh, the memories roll!

So here's to the prints with their sepia tones,
Each one a giggle, a smile, or a moan.
Faded and funny, forever we'll keep,
These gems of the past, they make memory leap.

Lanterns of Remembrance

On the porch, lanterns flicker and sway,
Each one whispers tales of a silly day.
A ghost from the attic, he wiggles his toes,
Says he once tickled the town's mayor's nose.

In the cupboard, old dishes start to chat,
One plate complains, it's a dog's chew toy mat.
The candles debate whose wax wears best,
While shadows perform their late-night jest.

A lantern hiccups, begins to spin,
Recalls that one time they lost to a pin.
The laughter can't stop, from the soft glowing light,
Remind us of moments that spark our delight.

So raise up your glass to these silly scenes,
Filled with the laughter of long-ago dreams.
For every dim bulb has a story be told,
Of dancing and prancing, of gaffes made bold.

The Echoing Footsteps

In hallways echoing with taps and squeaks,
Footsteps of laughter play hide-and-seek.
A pair of shoes that could tango and waltz,
Yet one always trips and walks into walls!

They march on the floorboards, a parading sound,
A comical echo that glides all around.
The cat turns to judge this ridiculous race,
Then pounces on socks in a dramatic chase.

Footsteps chase daylight from room to room,
Squeaking like mice, spreading giggles and gloom.
It's a silly ballet where no rules abide,
With pratfalls and stumbles and all turned aside.

So let them keep dancing, those echoes of cheer,
In a rhythm so silly, it's hard not to leer.
Each foot loves a joke, they twirl and they sway,
In a house full of laughter, they always will play.

Vestiges of a Fading Light

In corners of rooms where shadows conspire,
Dust bunnies plot, their ambitions inspire.
A moth with a flair for the bombastic ballet,
Spins a tale of curtains that used to sway.

The clock on the wall manipulates time,
Tick-tocks in rhythm, but dances out of rhyme.
It chuckles at hours that seem to go fast,
While slippers giggle at moments that passed.

With each fading beam, the laughter grows loud,
As beams play hide-and-seek underneath the cloud.
The shadows reach out to give a warm tease,
As the lights gently flicker and do as they please.

In this dance of the dimming, let joy have its say,
For laughter remains, where the silliness lay.
In a home where the echoes creep slowly at night,
We bask in the warmth of a fading light.

Flickering Moments

Time wobbles like jelly, oh what a sight,
Seconds are skipping, dancing in flight.
A clock tried a cartwheel, fell on the floor,
Now tick-tock is giggling, who could ask for more?

In corners, the shadows are playing charades,
Whispers of laughter in time's little trades.
A minute laughs loudly as it runs out the door,
Leaving behind only echoes and more.

The hour hand's teasing, it's sliding away,
Tickling the second, making it sway.
Each tick is a chuckle, each tock is a grin,
Oh, how this time game makes you want to spin!

As the pendulum swings, it's caught in a jest,
Racing with moments, who's winning? The quest!
A dance 'round the room, no worries, no stress,
Just time being silly, it's hard to suppress.

The Secrets of Old Doors

Old doors creak softly, their secrets unfold,
Whispers of laughter from ages of old.
Knobs that have giggled, hinges that sway,
Inviting the bold, there's mischief at play.

Behind every panel, a memory's peek,
A sock hop from fifty is feeling quite chic.
Polka dots scattered like confetti on cheer,
With stories of socks that have danced through the year.

Last night a doorknob began to sing loud,
An opera of echoes, it's drawing a crowd.
With each twist and turn, it chuckles with glee,
These doors are alive! Oh, how funny to see!

In a house full of memories, time's playful chase,
Old doors giggle gently, each yielding a space.
They jest with the moments, they laugh with a spin,
Revealing life's secrets hid deep within.

Diary of an Abandoned Space

In a dusty old attic, a diary sleeps tight,
With pages of giggles written in light.
Each chapter a chuckle, each line a delight,
It recounts a party that lasted all night.

Old shoes in the corner, they tango alone,
With a hat that once danced, now stuck to a bone.
The memories flutter like moths to a flame,
This space full of laughter remembers each name.

A chandelier giggles as dust falls like confetti,
Once bright as a star, now a tad bit unsteady.
But oh, what a night when the music played loud,
Walls were the witnesses, a very proud crowd.

Echoes still linger, they waltz in the beams,
In this abandoned space, nothing's as it seems.
The diary awakes with each story it tells,
Life was a comedy, oh, how it compels!

The Hourglass Nest

A nest made of moments, soft sands in the glass,
Time chirps like a bird, says, 'Hey, let's all pass!'
    Each grain is a giggle, a tiny delight,
    Swirling around in a fluttering flight.

What secrets they carry, these grains of the day,
Some dance in the wind while others just stay.
The hourglass chuckles, a wise little sage,
Saying, 'Time's just a jest, come join in the play!'

A flick of a wrist sends an avalanche down,
Moments tumble out, wearing laughter as crown.
Each second's a jester, each minute a tease,
Caught in this nest, it's a breeze if you please!

As the sands start to settle, a story is spun,
Of lighthearted mischief; it's all just for fun.
So gather your moments, let joy be your quest,
In this hourglass nest, you'll feel truly blessed.

Journey Through the Timelines

In a kitchen filled with yesterdays,
The bread still rises in funny ways.
Grandma's apron hangs up high,
She grins and winks, oh my, oh my!

The clock spins backward, what a sight,
We jump through ages with sheer delight.
Dancing on tables from years gone by,
Wobbling like jelly, and that's no lie!

A dinosaur roars, while wearing shades,
Sipping lemonade in a sunbeam parade.
We laugh and play with quirky minds,
In a land where no one really finds.

As the minutes play hide and seek,
Tickling memories, cheek to cheek.
We dive into laughter, soft and sublime,
Unraveling joy in the threads of time.

Echoes in the Hourglass

An hourglass full of dancing sand,
Whispers tales of a slapstick band.
Marbles roll down, one by one,
As we giggle at time, oh what fun!

Each grain a giggle, a story spun,
Of socks mismatched and a kid's bold run.
A cat in a hat, with a curious stare,
Chasing its tail without a care.

Flipping the hourglass, can you believe?
Tickling the past, we foolishly grieve.
As laughter echoes, no room for gloom,
We jam with joy in this tiny room!

A cupcake lands in the middle of the floor,
With sprinkles dancing, what's not to adore?
So we clap our hands and jump with glee,
In a world where time is just silly spree!

The Attic of Memories

In an attic where the dust bunnies roam,
Old trunks whisper secrets, finding a home.
A sock puppet battles a dinosaur,
As laughter echoes and spirits soar!

Old photos giggle in frames of gold,
Recounting stories both funny and bold.
A hat with a feather, slightly askew,
Wonders where all the youth went to!

Giant marbles are rolling all around,
Dancing to music that isn't even sound.
We play with our shadows, they lurch and flop,
As memories rise, they just can't stop!

In this nook of joy, time takes a break,
We leap through the past for laughter's sake.
So grab your imagination and take flight,
In the attic of fun, everything feels right!

Shadows on the Ticking Walls

Ticking and tocking, the shadows prance,
Waltzing to rhythms, they take a chance.
Silly hats tumble, with giggles in tow,
As we unravel the time, oh what a show!

The walls are alive with stories untold,
Of magic and mayhem, both funny and bold.
A mouse in a tuxedo, wearing a grin,
Challenges the clock to see who can win!

Time plays tricks in this wild escapade,
Where giggles and chuckles will never fade.
Shadows whisper secrets in playful rings,
A world of giggles, oh what joy it brings!

So let's tiptoe through clocks, leap and slide,
Celebrating moments where laughter can ride.
With shadows as friends, we dance and twirl,
In this tick-tocking land, let joy unfurl!

www.ingramcontent.com/pod-product-compliance
Lightning Source LLC
Chambersburg PA
CBHW051730290426
43661CB00122B/214